the S C I E N C E *library*

HUMAN BODY

the SCIENCE *library*

HUMAN BODY

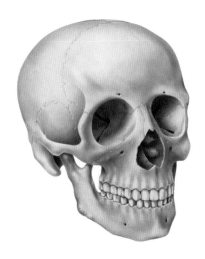

Steve Parker

Consultant: Dr Kristina Routh

Miles Kelly
PUBLISHING

First published in 2004 by Miles Kelly Publishing Ltd
Bardfield Centre Great Bardfield Essex CM7 4SL

Copyright©2004 Miles Kelly Publishing Ltd

This edition printed in 2008

2 4 6 8 10 9 7 5 3

British Library Cataloguing-in-Publication Data
A catalogue record for this book is available from the British Library

Editorial Director Belinda Gallagher
Art Director Jo Brewer
Editor Jenni Rainford
Editorial Assistant Chloe Schroeter
Cover Design Simon Lee
Design Concept Debbie Meekcoms
Design Stonecastle Graphics
Consultant Dr Kristina Routh
Indexer Hilary Bird
Reprographics Stephan Davis, Ian Paulyn
Production Manager Elizabeth Brunwin

ISBN 978-1-84236-991-3

Printed in China

www.mileskelly.net
info@mileskelly.net

www.factsforprojects.com

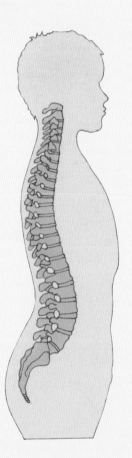

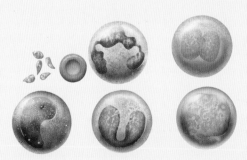

Contents

How to use this book

HUMAN BODY is packed with information, colour photos, diagrams, illustrations and features to help you learn more about science. Did you know that skin is the body's largest organ or that it takes more muscles to frown than it does to smile? Did you know that your brain weighs 1.4 kg or that the body makes 3 million new blood cells every second? Enter the fascinating world of science and learn about why things happen, where things come from and how things work. Find out how to use this book and start your journey of scientific discovery.

Main image
Each topic is clearly illustrated. Some images are labelled, providing further information.

Main text
Each page begins with an introduction to the different subject areas.

The grid
The pages have a background grid. Pictures and captions sit on the grid and have unique co-ordinates. By using the grid references, you can move from page to page and find out more about related topics.

To scale
This feature uses the grid to show comparative size of different objects. You can easily compare and see exactly how small or large things are.

Water and waste

24

THE BODY'S thousands of internal chemical processes, which work together, are known as its metabolism. This produces wastes of many kinds. Two main systems get rid of such body wastes. The digestive system removes not only bits of leftover and undigested food, but also some wastes of metabolism. The other waste disposal system is the urinary system whose main organs are the kidneys. They filter waste products, unwanted salts and water from the blood, and dispose of them in a watery fluid called urine. The amount of urine that is produced is controlled by hormones.

Adrenal gland

Right kidney

Inside the left kidney

Renal artery and vein

Major artery and vein

Ureter

▸ The urinary system controls the balance of water in the body.

Bladder

Urethra

● **Excretion and digestion**
About one-fifth of the blood pumped out by the heart (see pg21 [i25]) goes to the two kidneys. Inside each kidney are about 1 million tiny filters called nephrons. These take waste substances from the blood, along with excess water, to form urine. The urine flows down a tube, the ureter, to the bladder in the lower body. The bladder usually needs to be emptied, through the urethra, when it contains about 400 ml of urine. The solid wastes are removed from the end of the digestive tract through the anus. They contain mainly rubbed-off bits of intestine lining and undigested parts of food.

▸ Food takes about 48 hours to work its way through the digestive system.

Liver

Stomach

Gall bladder

Small intestine

Pancreas

Large intestine

Renal capsule (covering)

Anus

To scale
An adult ki... same size... glove – ab...

Read further › digestion pg22 [i13]

Renal artery brings blood to the kidney

Renal vein takes filtered blood away from the kidney

Ureter takes urine to the bladder

Outer layer or cortex containing nephrons (filters)

Inner layer or medulla

Adult ki...

▴ Inside the kidneys, the 1 million nephrons filter (clean) the blood.

The body consists of about two-thirds water – in an average adult that is a total of 40 to...

1 2 3 4 5 6 7 8 9 10 11 12 13 14 15 16

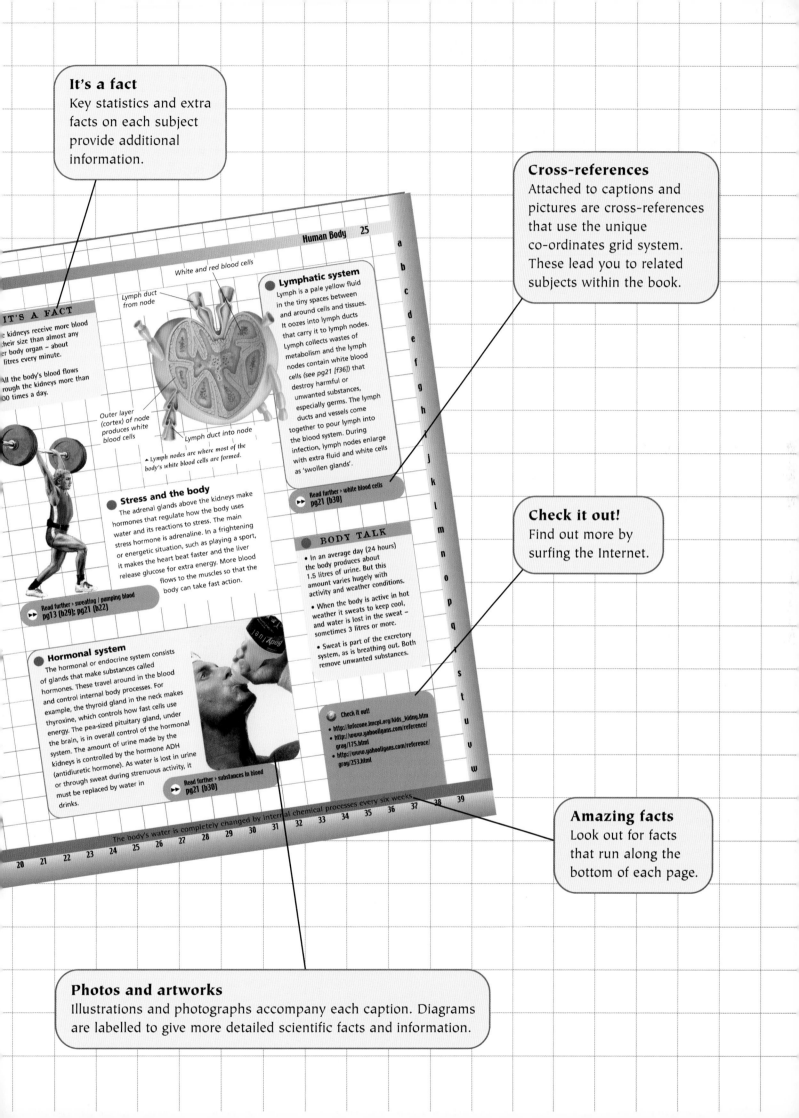

It's a fact
Key statistics and extra facts on each subject provide additional information.

Cross-references
Attached to captions and pictures are cross-references that use the unique co-ordinates grid system. These lead you to related subjects within the book.

Check it out!
Find out more by surfing the Internet.

Amazing facts
Look out for facts that run along the bottom of each page.

Photos and artworks
Illustrations and photographs accompany each caption. Diagrams are labelled to give more detailed scientific facts and information.

White and red blood cells

Lymph duct from node

IT'S A FACT

he kidneys receive more blood
heir size than almost any
r body organ – about
litres every minute.

All the body's blood flows
rough the kidneys more than
00 times a day.

Outer layer (cortex) of node produces white blood cells

Lymph duct into node

▲ Lymph nodes are where most of the body's white blood cells are formed.

Lymphatic system
Lymph is a pale yellow fluid in the tiny spaces between and around cells and tissues. It oozes into lymph ducts that carry it to lymph nodes. Lymph collects wastes of metabolism and the lymph nodes contain white blood cells *(see pg21 [f36])* that destroy harmful or unwanted substances, especially germs. The lymph ducts and vessels come together to pour lymph into the blood system. During infection, lymph nodes enlarge with extra fluid and white cells as 'swollen glands'.

▶▶ Read further > white blood cells
pg21 (b30)

Stress and the body
The adrenal glands above the kidneys make hormones that regulate how the body uses water and its reactions to stress. The main stress hormone is adrenaline. In a frightening or energetic situation, such as playing a sport, it makes the heart beat faster and the liver release glucose for extra energy. More blood flows to the muscles so that the body can take fast action.

▶▶ Read further > sweating / pumping blood
pg13 (b29); pg21 (b22)

BODY TALK

• In an average day (24 hours) the body produces about 1.5 litres of urine. But this amount varies hugely with activity and weather conditions.

• When the body is active in hot weather it sweats to keep cool, and water is lost in the sweat – sometimes 3 litres or more.

• Sweat is part of the excretory system, as is breathing out. Both remove unwanted substances.

Hormonal system
The hormonal or endocrine system consists of glands that make substances called hormones. These travel around in the blood and control internal body processes. For example, the thyroid gland in the neck makes thyroxine, which controls how fast cells use energy. The pea-sized pituitary gland, under the brain, is in overall control of the hormonal system. The amount of urine made by the kidneys is controlled by the hormone ADH (antidiuretic hormone). As water is lost in urine or through sweat during strenuous activity, it must be replaced by water in drinks.

▶▶ Read further > substances in blood
pg21 (b30)

Check it out!
• http://infozone.imcpl.org/kids_kidny.htm
• http://www.yahooligans.com/reference/gray/175.html
• http://www.yahooligans.com/reference/gray/253.html

The body's water is completely changed by internal chemical processes every six weeks

20 21 22 23 24 25 26 27 28 29 30 31 32 33 34 35 36 37 38 39

a b c d e f g h i j k l m n o p q r s t u v w

Body basics

WE KNOW more about the human body than anything else in the universe. Yet every day we find more detailed information about how the body moves, digests food, gets rid of wastes, controls its internal conditions, fights germs and disease, and stays fit and healthy. We make amazing discoveries about how the eyes see, how the ears hear, and how the brain thinks and learns. There are exciting new facts about the body's genetic information, made of DNA, which contains all the instructions for how the body grows, develops, carries out its life processes and survives in today's hazardous world.

Senses (see pg26 [k10]; pg27 [e28]; pg28 [l12])

Skin (see pg12 [t12])

Lungs (see pg18 [n13])

Digestive system (see pg24 [p15])

Heart (see pg21 [k25])

Joints (see pg15 [j35])

Bones (see pg14 [q15])

ORGANS	
Organ	Weight
• Skin	11,000 g
• Liver	1600 g
• Brain	1400 g
• Lungs	1100 g
• Heart	300 g

● Organs

The body is made of hundreds of different parts, including organs, muscles and bones. Organs are packed closely together – and they work with each other, too. They include lungs, liver (see pg23 [d35]), kidneys (see pg24 [e14]), stomach (see pg22 [r11]), eyes, ears, heart, blood (see pg21 [h32]), nerves (see pg31 [g30]) and brain (see pg32 [k14]), all wrapped up in the largest organ, the skin. Each of these organs, in turn, is made from millions of cells.

▶▶ Read further › cells
pg10 [g14]

Different outside, same inside

Human bodies have different sizes and shapes – women and men, girls and boys, old and young, wide and slim, dark and light, tall and short – with different clothes and hair styles. But inside, these bodies are almost identical. They all have the same inner parts, or organs, the same muscles and bones, and they work in the same way.

▶▶ Read further > DNA / organs
pg11 (b30); pg8 (j14)

Looking inside the living body

We can see inside living bodies in incredible detail, using various kinds of medical scanners. CT (computed tomography) and MRI (magnetic resonance imaging) scanners show details of the body tissues. PET (positron emission tomography) reveals how much energy is being used, especially in different parts of the brain, and can identify changes in cells that may cause disease.

▶▶ Read further > ultrasound
pg35 (b34)

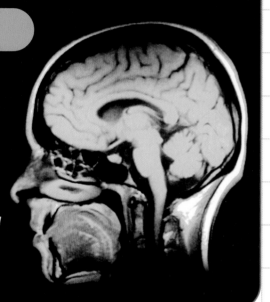

▸ MRI scans help diagnose diseases of the brain and nervous system. A computer builds a three-dimensional image using information from the scan.

IT'S A FACT

• Human beings are the most common large, living creatures on Earth.

• There are more than 6000 million humans in the world – far more than any kind of similar-sized animals such as lions, dolphins or even sheep.

• The world's oldest person is a Japanese woman aged about 115.

Social humans

Humans are social beings. Sometimes we want to be alone for a short time. But usually we like to be with other people, especially family and friends, as we talk, laugh and have fun together. In the fast-paced modern world, as we rush from place to place with less time to spare, the greatest fear of some people is being alone.

▶▶ Read further > smiling
pg17 (k33)

Check it out!
• http://www.howstuffworks.com/mri.htm
• http://www.kidinfo.com/Health/Human_Body.html

On average, people today live for 20 years longer than people did 100 years ago

a b c d e f g h i j k l m n o p q r s t u v w

The micro body

T HE HUMAN body is made of more than 50 million million microscopic cells. A typical cell is 0.02 mm across – about 1000 would fit on this full stop. There are at least 200 kinds of cells in the body, with different sizes and shapes, and different functions such as making products, moving substances around, delivering raw materials, collecting wastes or fighting germs. Most cells do not live for long. They wear out and die naturally at the rate of 50 million every second. However, specialized types of cells, called stem cells, are always dividing, to produce new cells that replace the old ones.

● Cells and organelles

The cell's outside layer is the plasma membrane. Inside, many tiny organelles (cells with specialized functions) float in the jelly-like cytoplasm. Sausage-shaped mitochondria break down glucose sugar to release its stored chemical energy, which powers the cell's processes. Ball-shaped ribosomes are like tiny factories making new substances, especially proteins, which are the cell's main structural parts or 'building bricks'.

►► Read further › cells / glucose / nourishment
pg11 (g22); pg25 (j26); pg31 (b34)

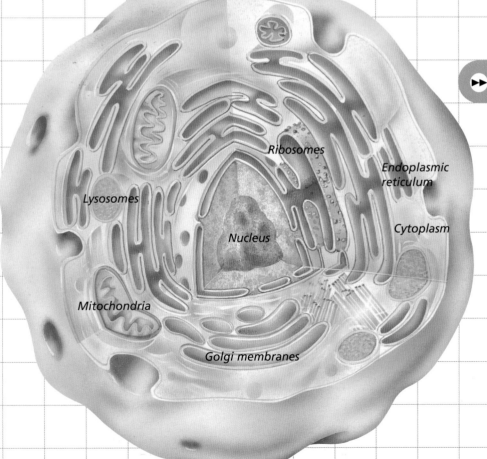

Plasma membrane

Ribosomes

Endoplasmic reticulum

Lysosomes

Cytoplasm

Nucleus

Mitochondria

Golgi membranes

◄ Inside a cell showing parts called organelles – cells with specialized functions.

● BODY TALK

• Most cells in the body live only a short time. A cell on the inside of the cheek lasts for about 10 hours. A cell on the surface of the skin lives for about 4 weeks, and a liver cell lasts 18 months.

• The longest-lived cells are nerve cells, which last for decades.

People once thought the human genome had millions of instructions or genes, but there are probably nearer to 35,000

Muscle layer

Elastic layer

Tough, outer cover

Inner lining

Plasma

Red cell

White cell

Platelets

Types of cells

Each kind of cell
is shaped to carry
out a particular function.
In blood, red cells are round and thin, to
absorb as much oxygen as possible through
their surface. Some white cells *(see pg21 [h34])*
are able to alter their shape to engulf germs.
The cells of the blood vessel lining are
flattened and joined to make a smooth layer.
Many cells of the same kind grouped together
are called a body tissue.

▼ *Red blood cells (seen under a microscope) are
disc-shaped. Each red blood cell contains almost
250 million haemoglobin molecules, which transport
oxygen around the body.*

Body instructions

The instructions that tell the body how to develop
its different parts and make them work together
are called the human genome. They are
inside each cell in the body, in the
form of the chemical DNA
(de-oxyribonucleic acid). The
whole genome contains 46
lengths of DNA. Until it
unravels to reveal its double
spiral shape, each is
coiled tightly to
form a thicker
structure – the
chromosome. There
are 46 chromosomes
inside the
nucleus of
each cell.

DNA coiled
into the
chromosome

Single
chromosome

DNA
unravelling

▶▶ **Read further › egg and sperm**
pg35 (k22)

DNA's
double
helix shape,
like a
twisted
rope ladder

Strands of DNA dividing
to make new copies

Strands are linked by
chemical subunits
called bases

New strands
are built
upon the
original ones

New strands
are identical
to the
original ones

Each of these
bases pairs up
with only one
other base

▶▶ **Read further › muscle / nerve cells**
pg17 (b22); pg31 (b34)

🌐 **Check it out!**

• http://www.bioanim.com
• http://www.biology.eku.edu/
RITCHISO/301notes1.htm

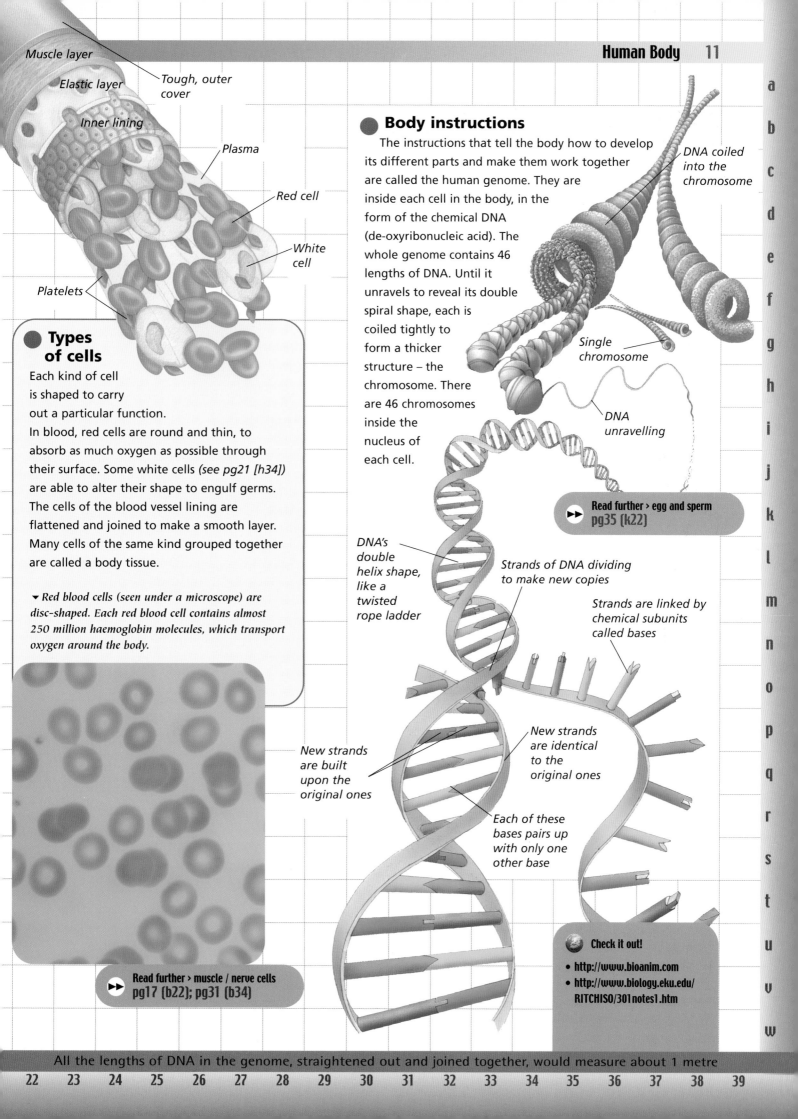

All the lengths of DNA in the genome, straightened out and joined together, would measure about 1 metre

a b c d e f g h i j k l m n o p q r s t u v w

Wrapped in skin

SKIN IS often said to 'glow with health'. In fact, its surface is dead. The surface of the skin is made of hard, toughened, flattened cells that have filled with the body protein keratin, and then died. They rub away and flake off in their thousands every minute as we move about, wear clothes, wash and dry with towels. Just under the surface, more cells are always multiplying, growing, filling with keratin and dying. They gradually move up to the surface to replace the old, worn-off skin. The whole cycle of skin replacement takes about four weeks.

IT'S A FACT

• Each year the body loses about 4 kg of rubbed-off skin flakes.

• The thinnest skin, on the eyelids, is only 0.5 mm thick.

• The sole of the foot has the thickest skin, up to 5 mm thick.

Read further › nerve signals pg31 (b34)

BODY TALK

• Human skin is very tough. It can repair many minor cuts and replace itself in grazes. But certain types of damage are more serious. In particular, too much strong sunshine is bad for skin.

• The sun's invisible rays, called UV-B (ultra-violet B), can harm the fast-dividing epidermal cells just under the skin's surface. This may cause a serious form of cancer called malignant melanoma. Clothing, a hat and sunscreen cream or lotion helps to shade and protect skin from powerful sunlight.

Under the surface

The upper layer of skin is called the epidermis. At its base are fast-multiplying cells that replace the old, keratin-hardened cells that rub off the surface. Under the epidermis is the thicker dermis. It contains strong, stretchy fibres of another body protein – collagen. The dermis also contains microscopic blood vessels (see pg21 pu32]), the growing bases or roots of hairs, sweat glands and nerves ending in micro-sensors to detect touch.

▼ Greatly enlarged view of skin showing its two main layers – epidermis and dermis.

Keratin layer of epidermis

Epidermis

Hair

Basal layer, of epidermis, where new cells grow

Hair erector muscle

Gland making oily sebum to keep hair and skin waterproof

Dermis

Hair root in follicle (pit)

Sweat gland

Nerve endings

Check it out!

• http://www.skin-information.com/
• http://www.kidshealth.org/kid/body/ skin_noSW.html

▸ *Microscopic view of a hair growing from its follicle.*

Hairs

Hairs, like skin, are dead. The only living part of a hair is at its base, where it grows in a tiny pit called a follicle (*see pg12 [u10]*). The upper part, or shaft, is made of old, dead, stuck-together hair cells. A hair on the head grows at a rate of about 3 mm each week. Body hairs grow slower; eyelash hairs grow much faster.

Read further > microscopic ear hairs
pg27 (b22)

Cool skin

Skin protects the softer, inner parts of the body from knocks and harm. It keeps in moist body fluids and keeps out dirt, germs and harmful substances such as strong chemicals. If the body is too hot, for example when exercising (*see pg25 [j24]*), tiny sweat glands in skin release watery sweat which oozes onto the surface of the skin. As sweat dries, it draws heat from the body and cools it.

Read further > sweat
pg25 (m34)

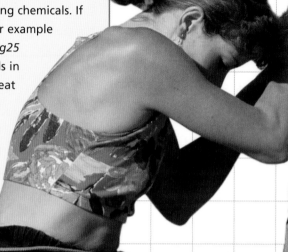

▸ *Sweating helps keeps the body at its correct temperature.*

Nails

A nail is hard, tough and dead, and made mainly of keratin. The only living part is its root, buried in the skin, which makes new nail tissue as the whole nail grows towards the fingertip or toetip. On average, fingernails lengthen about 2 mm each month. Toenails grow slightly slower. Both grow faster in summer. Nails form a stiff backing for the flexible fingertips and toetips, so we can feel, touch, sense pressure and grip.

▾ *Nails make fingertips strong enough to pluck guitar strings.*

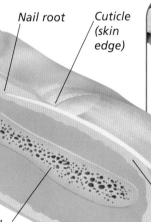

Nail root

Cuticle (skin edge)

Bone inside finger

Nail bed

Free edge of nail

Read further > skin and touch
pg28 (r8)

Joint effort

MORE THAN 200 bones form the body's internal supporting framework, called the skeleton. Bones are strong and stiff, giving the body its shape, protecting internal organs and holding together the soft parts such as blood vessels *(see pg21 [u30])*, nerves and guts. A single bone is rigid and tough, and can hardly bend. But the whole skeleton can move because its bones are linked at flexible joints, designed to reduce rubbing and wear. Bones are very strong, yet they are also very lightweight. They are made of active living tissue, so if they break because of too much pressure on them, they can usually repair themselves.

● Protection

Some bones protect very delicate body parts. For example, the skull bone protects the brain *(see pg32 [k14])* and main sense organs. All but one of the 22 bones in the skull – the mandible – are locked together to make the skull incredibly strong. Two deep bowl-like sockets called orbits, in the face, protect much of the eyeballs *(see pg26 [l9])*. The backbone, ribs and breastbone form a strong cage around the heart *(see pg21 [k26])* and lungs *(see pg18 [o11])*.

▶▶ **Read further › lungs / heart**
pg18 [m2]; pg21 [b22]

pg18 [m2]; pg21 [b22]

● IT'S A FACT

• There are 206 bones in the average skeleton.

• The longest bone in the body is the thighbone or femur, about one-quarter of the body's height.

• The smallest bone is the stirrup bone in the ear – it is only slightly bigger than this U.

Skull

Collarbone (Clavicle)

Breastbone (Sternum)

Upper arm bone (Humerus)

Rib

Backbone (Vertebrae)

Forearm (Ulna)

Radius

Sacrum

Hip bone (Pelvis)

Cranium

Thighbone (Femur)

Hand bones (Metacarpals)

Cheekbone (Zygoma)

Wrist bones (Carpals)

Orbit

Lower jaw (Mandible)

Kneecap (Patella)

Shinbone (Tibia)

Fibula

Ankle bones (Tarsals)

Foot bones (Metatarsals)

There is no truth in the old saying that men have one more pair of ribs than women – both usually have 12 pairs

Three layers

Most bones are not solid bone throughout. They have three layers. Outside is a 'shell' of hard or compact bone, which is very strong and stiff. Inside this is a layer of spongy or cancellous bone, with tiny holes for lightness. In the middle is marrow, a soft and jelly-like substance that makes new red and white cells for the blood. The whole bone is covered by a tough skin-like layer, the periosteum.

▸ *Bones grow and harden from birth to about the age of 20.*

Compact bone

Marrow

Spongy bone

Blood vessel

Osteon (rod-like subunit bone)

Periosteum

Read further › bone marrow
pg15 (q34)

▸ *The different parts of the knee joint work together to allow freedom of movement.*

Joints

Where bones meet in a joint, they are covered with a shiny, slightly softer substance known as cartilage, which is moistened by a slippery fluid (synovial fluid) that allows the joints to move smoothly. Ligaments are strips of strong tissue that hold bones together at the joints. Tendons are tough connective tissues that link bones to muscles (see pg16 [l6]).

Muscle

Kneecap (Patella)

Thighbone (Femur)

Ligament

Cartilage covers bone end

Tendon

Ligament

Cartilage pad

Shinbone (Tibia)

Read further › ball and socket
pg15 (m22)

Joint designs

The body has several different types of joints, which allow different kinds of movements. The hip is a ball-and-socket joint. The rounded end of the femur fits into a cup-shaped socket in the pelvis. This design allows lots of movements – up and down, side to side, and twisting. A hinge joint, such as the knee (see pg15 [j35]), can only move up and down. The elbow is also a hinge joint, which, along with the wrist joint, allows the hand to be turned with the palm facing up or down.

▸ *Gymnasts need supple, flexible joints to achieve extreme positions like this.*

Read further › muscles
pg16 (d2); pg17 (b22)

BODY TALK

• An adult's skeleton has 206 bones – but a baby's skeleton has over 340. This is because as the body grows, some separate bones join together to form one bone.

• Marrow is not found in all bones, and not all marrow is the same. In babies, nearly all bones contain red marrow (which makes new blood cells), but as the body grows some changes to yellow marrow (which stores fat).

But about one person in 20 has an extra two ribs – 13 pairs instead of 12

a b c d e f g h i j k l m n o p q r s t u v w

Muscle power

THE BODY'S 650 muscles make up almost half of its total weight. A typical muscle is striped, long and slim, bulging in the middle, and joined to a bone at each end. However, some muscles are shaped like triangles or sheets and may be joined to several bones, to each other, or not attached to bone, such as the layer of muscle in arteries. Muscles are designed to get shorter, or contract. As they contract, they pull on the bones they are attached to, and so move the body. The contraction of the muscles is controlled by nerve signals sent out from parts of the brain called the motor centres and cerebellum (see pg31 [t27]).

Trapezius turns head

Deltoid lifts arm

Biceps bends elbow

Latissimus dorsi pulls arm back and down (muscle at the back)

Rectus femoris (in front of thigh) straightens the knee

Extensor digitorum straightens fingers

IT'S A FACT

• Muscles make up about 45 per cent of male body weight; 40 per cent in a female.

• The biggest muscle is the gluteus maximus, in the buttocks.

• The smallest muscle is the stapedius, attached to the stirrup bone in the ear, which is the size of this dash —.

▼ A muscle is a bundle of thousands of myofibres that are grouped into bundles called fascicles.

Epimysium (outer covering)

Tapering end or head of muscle

Body or belly of muscle

Tendon

Actin (thin myofilament)

Myosin (thick myofilament)

● Layers of muscles

Just under the skin are dozens of muscles called the outer or superficial layer. Under these is usually another, intermediate layer, and there is also a third or deep muscle layer. Not all muscle actions cause movement. Several muscles may tense to hold a part steady and still (see pg15 [s30]). For example, when the body is standing, the neck and back muscles tense to keep it upright and balanced.

◀ Front superficial muscles.

Read further › joints
pg15 (m22)

Check it out!
• http://www.bioanim.com

It takes 42 muscles to frown, but only 18 to smile

To and fro

A muscle can forcefully pull or contract, but it cannot forcefully push or extend. So most muscles occur in pairs called antagonistic partners. One pulls the bone one way, and the other, on the opposite side of the bone, pulls the other way. Muscle pairs work together with other pairs as large muscle teams to move bones in many directions. When playing sport, our muscles are working in groups of pairs to respond to the moves we require.

Read further > face muscles
pg17 (k33)

◄ *More than 50 muscles work in each arm when playing sports such as volleyball.*

BODY TALK

• Muscles need energy to work. The energy needed comes from glucose, or blood sugar, which is carried by the blood.

• When a muscle is very active it needs much greater supplies of glucose. So the heart beats faster than normal and the blood vessels to the muscles widen, supplying the muscle with three times more blood than it has when it is at rest.

Fasciae enclose large groups of muscle fibres

Muscle fibres

A muscle contains bundles of long, thin muscle fibres (myofibres), about the width of human hairs *(see pg13 [b24])*. Each fibre is made of even thinner parts called muscle fibrils (myofibrils). And each fibril contains even narrower parts, myofilaments. There are two kinds of filaments, made of different types of protein: actin, which is thin, and myosin, which is thick. These slide past each other to shorten the fibrils, causing the whole muscle to contract.

Read further > muscle layers
pg16 (m9)

Nerve branches

Muscle fibres (myofibres)

Muscle fibril (myofibrils)

Face muscles

Most muscles pull on bones, and the bones work as long levers to move the skeleton *(see pg14 [l14])*. But in the face, several sets of muscles are joined to each other as well as to bones. There are seven muscles on each side of the mouth, which can pull it wider, up or down. More than 50 muscles are needed to make the facial expressions that show other people our thoughts and feelings.

Read further > bones and joints
pg14 (d2)

▶ *The muscles used to smile are called voluntary muscles because we can control how and when we use them, to express how we are feeling.*

A simple body movement like raising your arm uses more than 100 muscles

Take a breath

IN AN EMERGENCY, the human body can survive without food for several days, and even without water for a day or two. But it cannot survive without air for more than a few minutes. The air around us contains the gas oxygen. We cannot see, smell or taste oxygen. But it is needed for chemical changes inside the body, which break apart the high-energy substance glucose (blood sugar) obtained from food. The energy released from glucose powers almost all of the body's life processes. The parts specialized to take in air and pass oxygen from it into the blood, for spreading around the body, are known as the respiratory system.

● IT'S A FACT

• A pair of adult lungs holds about 3 litres of air.

• Opened out and laid out flat, the alveoli would cover an area about the size of half a soccer pitch.

▼ Inside the lungs, the bronchus divides into narrower bronchioles and again into even narrower alveoli.

● Respiratory system

The respiratory system consists of the nose, throat, larynx (voice box), trachea (windpipe), bronchi (main airways in the chest) and the lungs. Breathing in, or inspiring, draws fresh air into the lungs, where oxygen is taken in or absorbed into the blood *(see pg20 [h17])*. Breathing out, or expiring, causes the low-oxygen 'used air' to be pushed up along the airways and out of the body. The lungs' airways branch many times, becoming too thin to see. At the end of each branch is a group of microscopic air bubbles, called alveoli, surrounded by a network of equally tiny blood vessels, called capillaries. Oxygen seeps or diffuses from the air inside the alveoli, into blood in the capillaries, and is carried around the body.

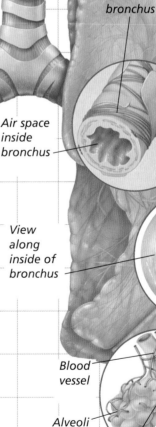

Trachea

Muscles in wall of bronchus

Right bronchus

Air space inside bronchus

View along inside of bronchus

Right lung

Blood vessel

Alveoli

Capillaries

Bronchiole

Air spaces in alveoli

▶▶ **Read further › blood vessels**
pg21 (p28)

● **Check it out!**
• http://www.kidinfo.com/Health/ Human_Body.html

After running a race, the body breathes five times faster than at rest

Absorbing oxygen

The main breathing muscle is the diaphragm, which is dome-shaped and sits under the lungs. When it tenses or contracts, it becomes flatter, expanding the lungs to suck in air. As the diaphragm relaxes again, the stretched lungs shrink back to their smaller size, pushing out air. Muscles between the ribs also contract when breathing in, to lift the front of the chest and help expand the lungs.

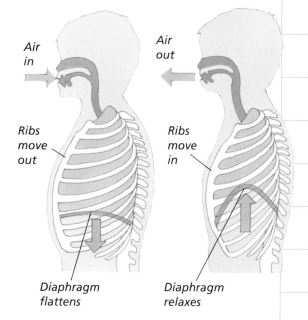

Air in

Air out

Ribs move out

Ribs move in

Diaphragm flattens

Diaphragm relaxes

Read further › muscle contraction
pg17 (b22)

Carrying air

There is no air in space, so astronauts must take their own supply of it. The air is contained in a special kind of backpack, which holds a main air tank and a reserve air tank. The main tank is connected to the astronaut's helmet. Whilst wearing the helmet, the astronaut is able to breathe in oxygen that is pumped into it from the tank. Chemicals inside the tank remove the carbon dioxide that is breathed out, to keep the air in the tank fresh.

Read further › waste disposal
pg25 (m34)

▸ *In order to breathe in space, astronauts have to carry tanks of oxygen.*

Vocal cords

Inside the larynx (voice box), in the front of the neck, two stiff ridges called vocal cords stick out from the sides. During normal breathing there is a triangle-shaped gap for air. To speak, muscles pull the ridges almost together. Air passing through the narrow gap makes them vibrate (shake to and fro rapidly), which produces sound.

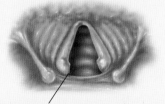

When the cords are apart, no sound is made as air can move freely past them

When the cords are pulled together by the laryngeal muscles, air is forced through a small gap and the cords vibrate to create a sound

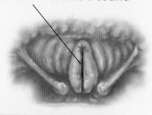

Read further › baby lungs
pg35 (r26)

BODY TALK

• The bulk of air, almost 79 per cent, is the gas nitrogen, which the body does not use. Fresh air when breathed into the body contains about 21 per cent oxygen and almost no carbon dioxide.

• After air has been in the lungs and breathed out, the proportion of carbon dioxide rises to 4 per cent. The proportion of oxygen falls to 15 per cent.

Heartbeat

BLOOD FLOWS round and round the body in a system of tubes called blood vessels. It is pumped by the heart, which has hollow chambers with strong muscular walls that contract to push the blood through the vessels. Blood carries many substances that are vital for life. These include oxygen and glucose (blood sugar) for energy, nutrients and raw materials for growth and repair, and natural body chemicals, called hormones, that control internal processes. At the same time, blood also takes away wastes and unwanted materials, including carbon dioxide, which is breathed out in the lungs.

The brain receives more blood for its size than any other part of the body

The pulmonary circulation takes blood to and from the lungs

Blood leaves the heart through a giant artery called the aorta

Blood returns to the heart through large veins called venae cavae

Radial artery

Iliac vein

Femoral artery

Saphenous vein

Peroneal artery

IT'S A FACT

• In most people, blood forms about one-twelfth (about 8 per cent) of the total body weight.

• An average adult man has a blood volume of 5 to 6 litres.

• An average adult woman has a blood volume of 4 to 5 litres.

• Compared to an adult, a baby has slightly less blood for its body size.

Circulatory system

The heart sends blood out into thick-walled vessels, called arteries. These branch and divide as they spread around the body, becoming thinner until they are microscopic blood vessels only one-hundredth of a millimetre across, called capillaries. Capillary walls are so thin that oxygen and other substances can easily diffuse (seep) out to the parts around. Capillaries join to make wider vessels, veins, that take blood back to the heart. On average, a drop of blood takes one minute to travel from the heart, through these vessels and back again. This movement is called the circulatory system.

Check it out!

• http://sln.fi.edu/biosci/heart.html

Read further > blood vessels
pg21 (p28)

Your body's blood vessels joined end to end would stretch twice round the Earth

1   2   3   4   5   6   7   8   9   10   11   12   13   14   15   16   17   18   19

Two pumps in one

The heart is not a single pump, but two, because the body has two circulations. The right side of the heart sends blood through the pulmonary circulation to the lungs *(see pg18 [m14])*, to pick up supplies of oxygen. This blood returns to the left side of the heart, which pumps it all around the body in the systemic circulation, to deliver the oxygen. The blood comes back to the heart again to continue its endless journey.

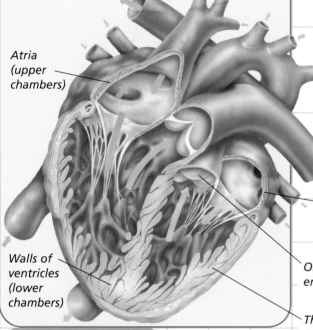

Atria (upper chambers)

Walls of ventricles (lower chambers)

Thin walls of atria stretch as blood enters from the veins

One-way valves inside the heart ensure blood flows the correct way

Thick muscular ventricle walls contract to push blood into the arteries

▶▶ **Read further > lungs**
pg19 [b22]

A complex liquid

About half of blood is a watery fluid, plasma, with glucose, hormones and many other substances dissolved in it. The other half is composed of cells. There are three main types: red cells carrying oxygen, white cells to fight disease, and platelets to help blood to clot and seal a wound. One cubic mm of blood (the size of a pinhead) contains 5 million red cells, 8000 white cells and 350,000 platelets.

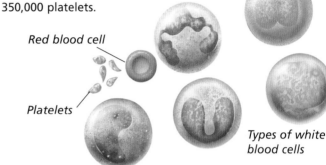

Red blood cell

Platelets

Types of white blood cells

▲ *There are two main types of white blood cell: monocytes that surround and digest germs, and lymphocytes that use antibodies to destroy germs.*

▶▶ **Read further > cells / lymph nodes**
pg10 [d2]; pg11 [g22]; pg25 [b34]

▼ *Veins are wide and their walls are thin and floppy.*

Inner lining (endothelium)

Valve in vein

Elastic layer

BODY TALK

• The heartbeat rate is measured in the wrist as the pulse rate, and it varies with age and activity. A new baby's average rate is 120 to 130 per minute, even when asleep. By about the age of seven years old, this average resting rate has fallen to 80 to 90. In the adult body, the rate is around 70.

• During hard exercise, such as running a race, the adult pulse rate can double, up to about 140.

Blood vessels

Arteries have thick, stretchy walls to cope with pressure as blood surges out of the heart at high speed. Each heartbeat makes the arteries bulge all through the body. The bulge or pulsation is felt easily in the wrist as the pulse. Capillary walls are only one cell thick. Veins carry slow-moving, low-pressure blood. Because blood moves so slowly, many veins, particularly in the legs, have valves to stop blood from flowing the wrong way.

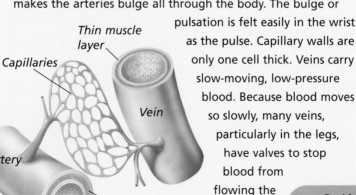

Thin muscle layer

Capillaries

Vein

Artery

Thick muscle layer

▶▶ **Read further > blood**
pg21 [b30]

a b c d e f g h i j k l m n o p q r s t u v w

Eating for life

THE BODY takes in a huge range of foods including meat and fish, bread, rice and pasta, and fresh fruits and vegetables. But the journey for all these foods is the same. They pass into the digestive tract, which is a passageway looped and coiled within the body. As foods pass along the tract they are broken down or digested into smaller, simpler substances, called nutrients, which can be absorbed into the blood stream. The whole journey for food, from one end of the tract to the other, lasts up to 48 hours.

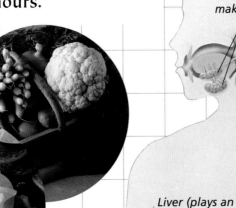

▲ A balanced diet including fresh vegetables, for essential minerals, and carbohydrate, for energy, is vital for a healthy digestive system.

Check it out!
- http://www.geocities.com/Area 51/Dunes/9641/digestive.htm
- http://www.borg.com/~lube hawk/hdigsys.htm

IT'S A FACT
- In an adult the whole digestive tract is about 9 m long.
- The longest part of the digestive system is the small intestine, measuring 6 m.
- The large intestine is about 1.5 m long.

Digestive system
In the mouth, foods are chewed and moistened by saliva (spit). They are swallowed down the oesophagus (gullet) into the stomach, and are churned around with gastric juices that contain chemicals called acids and enzymes. These enzymes turn food into a thick soup-like substance, called chyme, which oozes into the small intestine. Here nutrients are absorbed into the blood. Waste products are stored in the rectum and leave the body through the anus.

▶▶ Read further › excretory system pg24 (m2)

BODY TALK
- During a large meal the stomach stretches to hold about 1.5 litres of chewed food. Its lining makes a powerful acid – hydrochloric acid – to attack and digest food. This acid also helps to kill germs (harmful microbes) in the food.
- The stomach does not digest its own lining because it is coated with a layer of slimy mucus, which resists the acid attack.

Three pairs of salivary glands make saliva

Swallowed food goes down the oesophagus (gullet)

Liver (plays an important role in processing digested food)

Stomach

Pancreas (secretes pancreatic juices)

Large intestine

Small intestine

Appendix

Rectum

Anus

The stomach and the pancreas both make about 2 litres of digestive juices daily

1 2 3 4 5 6 7 8 9 10 11 12 13 14 15 16 17 18 19

Liver

The liver is not part of the digestive tract, but it is part of the digestive system. It receives nutrient-rich blood from the small intestine. The liver makes a green liquid called bile, which breaks down fatty foods. Bile is stored in the gall bladder. To the left of the liver and behind the stomach is another digestive organ, the pancreas. It produces powerful enzymes to aid food breakdown in the small intestine.

▶▶ Read further > digestion / waste
pg22 (i13); pg24 (m2)

Left lobe

Right lobe

Dividing ligament

Hepatic artery (brings oxygen-rich blood from the heart)

Bile duct

Gall bladder

Hepatic portal vein (carries food-rich blood from the small intestine)

▼ Inside a tooth, many blood vessels and nerves pass through the pulp into the jaw bone.

Enamel Dentine

Pulp

Gum

Root canal

Jaw bone

Blood vessels and nerves

Small intestine

Most nutrients are absorbed through the small intestine lining into the blood flowing through its walls. The lining is folded into ridges called plicae, and the surfaces of the plicae are also folded, into tiny finger-like structures about 1 mm tall, called villi. Similarly, the surface of each villus is covered with thousands of microvilli. The plicae, villi and microvilli give a huge surface area for absorbing nutrients – more than 20 times the body's whole skin area.

Blood vessels inside villus

Villus

Plicae

Wall of intestine

▸ Villi line the intestine.

▶▶ Read further > digestive system
pg22 (i13)

Teeth

A person has 52 teeth, but not at the same time. The first (baby) set appear soon after birth and number 20. These deciduous teeth begin to fall out when children are about six years old, and are replaced by the second (adult) or permanent set of 32 teeth. Each tooth is covered by enamel (see pg23 [i23]), the hardest substance in the body. Under the enamel is slightly softer dentine. The centre of the tooth has a living pulp of blood vessels and nerves.

First incisor

Second incisor

Canine

First and second premolars

First and second molars

Third molar (wisdom tooth)

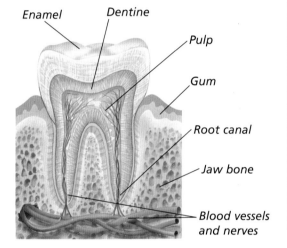

▲ The adult teeth in one half of the lower jaw.

▶▶ Read further > blood vessels
pg21 (p28)

To scale
Each square of the grid = 1 cm

Average baby molar tooth is 0.5 cm

Average adult molar tooth is 1.5 cm

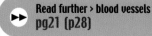
The liver is the largest internal organ, and weighs about 1.5 kg

Water and waste

THE BODY'S thousands of internal chemical processes, which work together, are known as its metabolism. This produces wastes of many kinds. Two main systems get rid of such body wastes. The digestive system removes not only bits of leftover and undigested food, but also some wastes of metabolism. The other waste disposal system is the urinary system whose main organs are the kidneys. They filter waste products, unwanted salts and water from the blood, and dispose of them in a watery fluid called urine. The amount of urine that is produced is controlled by hormones.

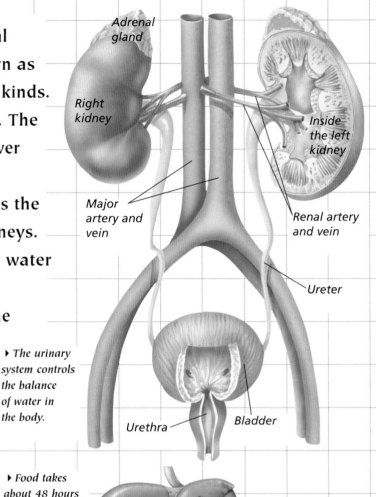

Adrenal gland

Right kidney

Inside the left kidney

Major artery and vein

Renal artery and vein

Ureter

▶ *The urinary system controls the balance of water in the body.*

Urethra

Bladder

● Excretion and digestion

About one-fifth of the blood pumped out by the heart *(see pg21 [i25])* goes to the two kidneys. Inside each kidney are about 1 million tiny filters called nephrons. These take waste substances from the blood, along with excess water, to form urine. The urine flows down a tube, the ureter, to the bladder in the lower body. The bladder usually needs to be emptied, through the urethra, when it contains about 400 ml of urine. The solid wastes are removed from the end of the digestive tract through the anus. They contain mainly rubbed-off bits of intestine lining and undigested parts of food.

▶▶ **Read further › digestion**
pg22 (i13)

▶ *Food takes about 48 hours to work its way through the digestive system.*

Liver

Stomach

Gall bladder

Pancreas

Small intestine

Large intestine

Anus

Renal artery brings blood to the kidney

Renal capsule (covering)

Renal vein takes filtered blood away from the kidney

Outer layer or cortex containing nephrons (filters)

Ureter takes urine to the bladder

Inner layer or medulla

▲ *Inside the kidneys, the 1 million nephrons filter (clean) the blood.*

To scale
An adult kidney is about the same size as a small boxing glove – about 6 cm long

Adult kidney

Boxing glove

IT'S A FACT

• The kidneys receive more blood for their size than almost any other body organ – about 1.2 litres every minute.

• All the body's blood flows through the kidneys more than 300 times a day.

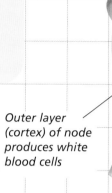

White and red blood cells

Lymph duct from node

Outer layer (cortex) of node produces white blood cells

Lymph duct into node

▲ *Lymph nodes are where most of the body's white blood cells are formed.*

Stress and the body

The adrenal glands above the kidneys make hormones that regulate how the body uses water and its reactions to stress. The main stress hormone is adrenaline. In a frightening or energetic situation, such as playing a sport, it makes the heart beat faster and the liver release glucose for extra energy. More blood flows to the muscles so that the body can take fast action.

Read further › sweating / pumping blood
pg13 (b29); pg21 (b22)

Lymphatic system

Lymph is a pale yellow fluid in the tiny spaces between and around cells and tissues. It oozes into lymph ducts that carry it to lymph nodes. Lymph collects wastes of metabolism and the lymph nodes contain white blood cells *(see pg21 [f36])* that destroy harmful or unwanted substances, especially germs. The lymph ducts and vessels come together to pour lymph into the blood system. During infection, lymph nodes enlarge with extra fluid and white cells as 'swollen glands'.

Read further › white blood cells
pg21 (b30)

BODY TALK

• In an average day (24 hours) the body produces about 1.5 litres of urine. But this amount varies hugely with activity and weather conditions.

• When the body is active in hot weather it sweats to keep cool, and water is lost in the sweat – sometimes 3 litres or more.

• Sweat is part of the excretory system, as is breathing out. Both remove unwanted substances.

Hormonal system

The hormonal or endocrine system consists of glands that make substances called hormones. These travel around in the blood and control internal body processes. For example, the thyroid gland in the neck makes thyroxine, which controls how fast cells use energy. The pea-sized pituitary gland, under the brain, is in overall control of the hormonal system. The amount of urine made by the kidneys is controlled by the hormone ADH (antidiuretic hormone). As water is lost in urine or through sweat during strenuous activity, it must be replaced by water in drinks.

Read further › substances in blood
pg21 (b30)

Check it out!

• http://infozone.imcpl.org/kids_kidny.htm

The body's water is completely changed by internal chemical processes every six weeks

Sight and sound

MORE INFORMATION about the outside world enters the body through the eyes and ears – from pictures, noises, words on paper and everyday sounds – than through all the other senses combined. All the body's sense organs work in the same way. They detect changes or features, and produce patterns of tiny nerve signals that are sent to the brain (*see pg32 [l10]*). The eye detects light as rays of different colours and brightness. The ear detects vibrations of sound that reach it as invisible air waves.

▶ *Light enters the eye through the pupil. It then travels through the cornea and lens to form an image on the retina at the back of the eye.*

Optic chiasma where signals from each eye partly cross over

Retina – the lining of light-sensitive rods and cones

Choroid layer

Sclera (covering)

Iris

Ligaments supporting the lens

Lens

Optic nerve which carries the signals to the brain

Cornea

Tear fluid gland

Muscles that turn the eye

Pupil

Iris

Tear duct in to nose

Outer sheath of eyeball (sclera)

▶▶ **Read further › visual area pg32 [n15]**

Check it out!

• http://www.kidinfo.com/health/ Human_Body.html

Inside the eye

The eyeball, about 2.5 cm across, has a tough outer cover, the sclera. At the front is a transparent window, the dome-shaped cornea, which lets in light rays. These pass through the lens that bends (refracts) them to shine a clear image of the world on to the retina lining the eyeball. Here, millions of light-sensitive cells change the patterns of light into nerve signals. The eye's retina has two kinds of light-sensitive cells. Rods are tall and slim, and number about 125 million. They detect shades of light and work well in dim light but cannot see colours. The 7 million cones are shorter and wider and clustered at the rear where the central part of the image falls. They see colours and fine details in bright light.

In perfect darkness, a healthy eye can see a candle flame 3 km away

a
b
c
d
e
f
g
h
i
j
k
l
m
n
o
p
q
r
s
t
u
v
w

Inside the ear

Sound waves pass into a slightly S-shaped tube, the outer ear canal, and hit the small, flexible eardrum at the end. The vibrations pass along three tiny bones – the hammer, anvil and stirrup – and into the fluid inside the snail-shaped cochlea. The vibrations cause ripples that are sensed by microscopic hairs on auditory cells, and then changed into nerve signals.

Outer ear (pinna)

Sound wave

Outer ear canal

Hammer

Anvil

Stirrup

Eustachian tube

Semicircular canals (balance)

Eardrum

Cochlea

Layers of hair cells in fluid inside the cochlea

Read further › nerve signals
pg31 (b22)

Eye colour

The coloured part of the eye is the iris – a ring of muscle seen through the clear cornea. The dark hole in the middle of the iris is the pupil, where light passes to the inside of the eye. Nearly all babies are born with blue eyes. After a few months the colour may change to a shade of brown, green or grey, then it stays the same. This colour is inherited from parents. If the mother and father are both blue-eyed, their child will almost certainly have blue eyes. However, if one or both parents are brown-eyed, then their child may have brown or blue eyes.

Parents' eye colour

Genes for eye colour

Possible colours for children

Read further › babies' genes
pg35 (k22)

Three ossicles

The three ear bones known as the ossicles are the hammer, anvil and stirrup. These are the smallest bones in the body. Surrounding muscles tense to hold them firmly so that they vibrate less when very loud sound waves hit them. These muscles prevent too-loud sounds damaging the ear. The eustachian tube controls the air pressure inside the ear by letting air in and out. The eustachian tube can be opened up by yawning or swallowing.

Laser surgery

A narrow beam of high-power laser light can be shone accurately into the eye, to carry out treatment for various eye disorders. The heat from the beam can seal a leaky blood vessel, or sculpt and reshape the lens (see pg26 [l18]) and cornea (see pg26 [m19]) to make vision clearer.

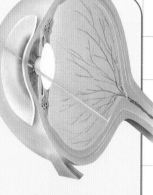

▲ Laser surgery on the retina can mean that spectacles or contact lenses are no longer needed.

Read further › inside the eye
pg26 (o13)

A sound detected by the brain reaches one ear 1/1500th of a second before it reaches the other ear

Smell, taste and touch

BOTH SMELL and taste are chemo-senses. They detect tiny particles of chemical substances – odorants floating in the air, and flavorants in foods and drinks. The two senses work separately, but they usually both send messages to the brain at the same time, when we eat and drink. So does the sense of touch, as the lips, tongue, gums and cheeks detect the temperature and hardness or consistency of the food. Smell, taste and touch are all closely linked or associated in the brain (see pg32 [j13] – especially when we eat. What we imagine as the 'taste' of a meal is really a combination of these three senses.

Olfactory bulb

Olfactory tract to brain

Scent-sensitive cells of olfactory epithelium

Mucus lining (inside nose)

Hard palate (roof of mouth)

Nostril

▲ Scent particles dissolve in the mucus lining. The cells at the top of the nose then send signals along the olfactory nerve to the brain.

▶▶ Read further > types of cells
pg11 (g22)

● Inside the nose

The sensory parts for smell are two patches called olfactory (smell) epithelia. They are in the roof of the nasal chamber, inside the skull bone behind the nose. Each patch contains millions of olfactory cells (see pg29 [s25]), which have bunches of micro-hairs, cilia. These detect certain odorant particles from the air that float into the nose and land on them.

Epidermis

Keratin layer

Pain sensors

Light touch sensors

Heavy pressure sensors

● Skin and touch

The sense of touch uses microscopic sensors at the ends of nerve fibres in the dermis, just under the surface of the skin (see pg12 [r12]), to detect a range of physical contacts. These include light touch and heavy pressure, heat and cold, and movements or vibrations. In the fingertips there are 10,000 micro-sensors in every square millimetre of skin.

▶▶ Read further > dermis layer of skin
pg12 (i11)

▲ Some of the microscopic sensors found within the skin.

An olfactory or smell cell in the nose lives for 30 days

Tongue and taste

The front, sides and rear of the tongue have thousands of taste buds set into the surface, scattered between the larger 'lumps' called papillae. Each taste bud is one-tenth of a millimetre across. It contains about 25 gustatory (taste) cells, which have tufts of micro-hairs called cilia. These detect chemical flavouring particles in food. The tip of the tongue is most sensitive to sweet tastes, the front sides to salty, the rear sides to sour, and the middle rear to bitter tastes.

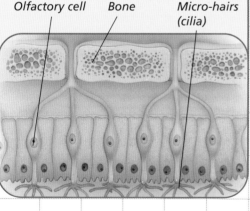

Smaller papillae · Large papillae · Taste buds · Inner tongue layers

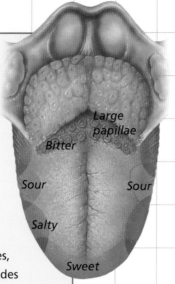

Large papillae · Bitter · Sour · Sour · Salty · Sweet

▲ The tongue has many taste buds to detect different flavours but its main upper surface has no taste buds.

Read further > chewing food
pg22 (i13)

BODY TALK

• The body has five main senses: sight (visual), hearing (auditory), smell (olfactory), taste (gustatory) and touch (somato–sensory), but there are millions of other tiny sensors inside the body too.

• Sensors in the inner parts of the ear detect the head's position and movements, while those in muscles and joints bring information about the position of the body and limbs. This helps us to keep our balance and posture.

• Other micro–sensors detect internal body conditions such as temperature and blood pressure.

▼ Smells are scent molecules which are taken into your nose by breathed-in air. A particular smell may be noticeable even when mixed with millions of air molecules.

Smell cells

Olfactory cells have micro-hairs or cilia facing down into the nasal chamber, which detect smell particles landing on them. These particles drift into the nose with breathed-in air and move into the nasal chamber.

Olfactory cell · Bone · Micro-hairs (cilia)

Sensing smells and tastes

It is not clear how the micro-hairs, or cilia, on smell and taste cells respond to chemical particles. It is possible that the surfaces of the cilia have tiny pits in them of different shapes. A certain odorant or flavorant particle fits into one shape of pit, but not the others – like a key into its lock. Only when the particle fits properly, is a nerve signal sent to the brain.

Read further > nerve signals
pg31 (b22)

Nerves all over

THE BODY consists of many different organs and tissues. These must work together in an organized way for the whole body to stay healthy and active. The main system that controls and co-ordinates all these parts is the nervous system. Like a computer network, it sends tiny electrical signals to and fro, carrying information from one part of the body to another. The electrical signals are called nerve messages and they travel along wire-like nerves, which spread in a vast network through the entire body. Central control of the whole nervous system and the whole body comes from the brain (see pg32 [k14]).

Brain
Cranial nerve
Spinal cord
Brachial plexus (nerve junction)
Intercostal nerve
Lumbar nerves
Sacral nerve
Radial nerve
Ulna nerve
Sciatic nerve
Tibial nerve
Peroneal nerve
Lateral plantar nerve

IT'S A FACT

• The spinal cord is about 45 cm long and 31 pairs of main peripheral nerves branch from it.

• The thickest peripheral nerve is the sciatic nerve in the lower hip and upper thigh – almost as wide as a thumb.

▶ The spinal cord is the bundle of nerves running down the middle of the backbone.

Spinal cord
Backbone

Check it out!

• http://ghs.gresham.k12.or.us/ science/ps/sci/ibbio/Anatomy/ nervous/neuron.htm

The nervous system

The nervous system has three main parts: brain, spinal cord and peripheral nerves. The brain consists of billions of nerve cells and other tissues in the top half of the head. Its lower end merges into the spinal cord, the body's main nerve. The spinal cord is inside a tunnel formed by the row of holes inside the vertebrae of the backbone or spine. Peripheral nerves branch out from the spinal cord and brain to reach every body part.

▶▶ Read further › bones and joints pg15 [b34; m22]

Some nerve cells have synapses (links) with 250,000 other nerve cells

Nerve cells

The nervous system is built up of billions of very specialized cells called nerve cells or neurons. Each has many spider-like branches, called dendrites, that receive signals from other nerve cells. The signals pass out along the nerve fibre, or axon, to other nerve cells. Nerve fibres are too thin to see with the unaided eye. But some nerve cells are more than 30 cm in length, making them some of the longest cells in the body.

▶▶ Read further > waste removal
pg24 (m2)

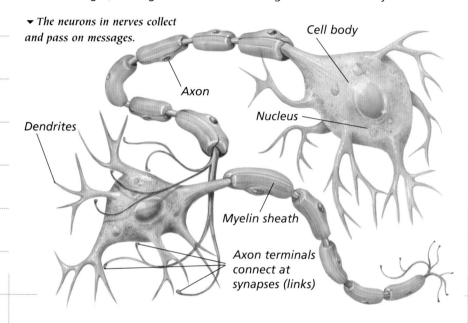

▾ *The neurons in nerves collect and pass on messages.*

Cell body

Axon

Nucleus

Dendrites

Myelin sheath

Axon terminals connect at synapses (links)

How the brain works

Nine-tenths of the brain consists of the cerebrum, composed of two large, dome-shaped, wrinkled parts called cerebral hemispheres *(see pg32 [j13])*. At the lower rear is a smaller wrinkled part, the cerebellum *(see pg32 [n12])*. It makes muscle-powered movements smooth, skilful and co-ordinated. The central parts of the brain, such as the thalamus, are involved in awareness, memories and emotions. The lowest part is the brain stem, which is responsible for automatic body processes such as digestion and heartbeat.

Thalamus affects sensory levels, awareness and alertness

Cerebrum is the site of mental activity such as thinking and learning

Limbic system affects body functions and emotions

Hippocampus, linked to mood, willpower, learning and memory

Cerebellum controls co-ordination

Hypothalamus controls body heat, water and hunger, and wakes you up

Brain stem controls heartbeat and breathing

▶▶ Read further > the brain
pg32 (n15)

Inside a nerve

A nerve has a tough, shiny, greyish covering, called the epineurium. Inside are bundles, or fascicles, of nerve fibres that carry the tiny electrical pulses of nerve signals. A thick nerve has hundreds of thousands of fibres, while the thinnest nerves, as fine as a human hair, have just a few. Also inside the nerve are small blood vessels *(see pg21 [u30])* to bring nourishment and take away wastes. Nerve signals travel so fast that we can sense a situation and react to it in less than 0.2 seconds.

▾ *Nerves allow us to have split-second reactions – essential for sports such as snowboarding.*

▶▶ Read further > types of cells
pg11 (g22)

BODY TALK

• Different types of nerve fibres carry signals at different speeds. The fastest signals travel at more than 120 m per second.

• The slowest signals travel at 1–2 m per second.

Awake, asleep, a dream

THE BRAIN is the site of the human mind. It is where we think, imagine, receive information from our senses, work out what it means, make decisions, store memories, experience emotions, such as fear and happiness, and control body movements. Most of these processes happen in the cerebral cortex – the thin, grey layer that covers the domed, wrinkled surface of the brain. Some processes, such as creating a picture in the mind of what the eyes see, happen mainly in one part of the cortex. Other processes, such as storing and recalling memories, involve several areas of the cortex and also other parts of the brain.

Touch

Movement (motor)

Awareness

Speech

Hearing

Cerebellum (movement co-ordination)

Vision

▲ Different areas or centres of the brain's cortex deal with different processes and body parts.

BODY TALK

• The two halves (hemispheres) of the brain look the same, but they work in different ways. In most people, the left hemisphere is important in using numbers and words, working out problems in a logical way, planning, reasoning and comprehension.

• The right hemisphere deals with recognizing patterns in shapes, colours and sounds, imagination and having ideas and inspiration.

Check it out!

• http://www.yahooligans.com/ reference/gray/186.html

Control areas

The visual centre or area of the brain is at the lower rear of the cortex and receives nerve signals from the eyes (see pg26 [h11]) and works out what is seen. The movement or motor centre controls the body movements by making muscles contract and relax (see pg17 [m22]). The touch centre just behind the motor centre receives signals from the skin about what is felt on different parts of the body surface.

▶▶ Read further › muscle control pg16 [m9]

The whole brain weighs about 1.4 kg

1 2 3 4 5 6 7 8 9 10 11 12 13 14 15 16 17 18 19

Seeing thoughts

▶▶ Read further › nerves
pg30 (m8)

Billions of nerve signals *(see pg30 [k15])* flash around the brain every second, bringing information from the senses, sending out instructions to the muscles, and carrying thoughts and memories. Some of the signals 'leak' through the skull bone to the body's surface, where they can be picked up by sensor pads on the skin. These signals can be detected by a machine called an electroencephalograph (EEG) and displayed as spiky, wavy lines called an electroencephalogram.

When the body sleeps

Most people sleep about seven to eight hours each night; newborn babies *(see pg35 [p36])* need as much as 20 hours of sleep a day. Each night, when we first go to sleep, it is very deep with relaxed muscles and slow breathing and heartbeat. Then comes a period of light or REM sleep (REM means 'rapid eye movement') where the muscles twitch, breathing and heartbeat speed up, and the eyes flick to and fro even though the eyelids are closed. Short periods of REM sleep alternate with long periods of deep sleep, causing the deep sleep to get shallower until waking.

▶▶ Read further › newborn babies
pg35 (r26)

◄ *Most of the body's basic activities slow down as we sleep, but the brain stays active all night receiving sense signals.*

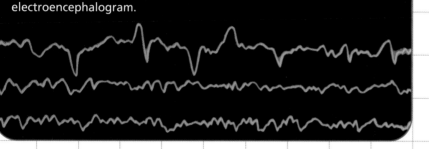

Most muscles are relaxed and floppy

Breathing is slower

Digestive parts work more slowly

Heartbeat is slower

Kidneys produce less urine

I saw it in a dream

People who wake up during or just after REM sleep usually say they have been dreaming. Recordings from EEG machines *(see pg33 [g26])* show that the brain is very active during this time. Dreams may occur when the brain recalls recent events and makes new memories out of them. However, dreaming can also bring unusual ideas, which are not restricted by the real world of being awake. Dreaming or daydreaming is a time when many artists and creative people have their best ideas.

The Angel of the North, Gateshead, UK

◄ *Works of art can be the realization of an artist's dream or daydream.*

▶▶ Read further › brain activity
pg31 (m22)

The folds and wrinkles of the brain surface, spread out flat, would cover the area of a pillowcase

Making babies

EVERY SECOND, another three human beings enter the world. They are new babies, born after nine months of growing and developing inside their mothers. The parts of the body that produce new human beings are known as the reproductive system. The reproductive parts are the only body system that is not fully formed and working at birth. The reproductive system completes its development around the ages of 11 to 13 in girls, and 14 to 16 in boys, which is the time known as puberty. The process of reproduction begins with the joining of two single cells – the egg from the mother, and the sperm from the father.

▾ *Babies grow inside the womb for around 40 weeks (9 months), before they are born.*

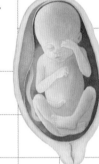

24 weeks

20 weeks

16 weeks

12 weeks

8 weeks

● Female reproductive parts

The egg cell is relatively large, 0.1 mm across. The main female sex organs, the ovaries, contain many thousands of egg cells. Every month one egg becomes ripe and is released into the oviduct or egg tube (fallopian tube) in a process called ovulation. It passes along the tube, where it may meet a sperm cell *(see pg35 [r24])* and be fertilized *(see pg35 [j29])*.

▶▶ Read further > sperm cell
pg34 (q13)

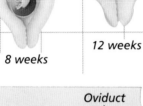

Ovary
Oviduct
Uterus
Cervix
Vagina

▲ *Female reproductive parts.*

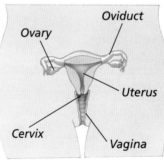

Erectile tissue
Urethra
Vas deferens
Bladder
Scrotum
Testis
Penis

▲ *Male reproductive parts (side view).*

● Male reproductive parts

Compared to the egg cell, the sperm cell is tiny, just 0.05 mm long. The main male sex organs, the testes, make millions of them each day and they live for about 1 month. If the sperm cells do not pass along the ductus deferens or sperm tube, and then out of the body through the penis, they gradually die and break apart as new ones form.

▶▶ Read further > egg cell
pg34 (m2)

▸ *Between 32 and 36 weeks, the baby usually turns in the womb, ready to be born head first.*

Umbilical cord

36 weeks

32 weeks

Placenta

28 weeks

40 weeks

Cervix (neck of the womb)

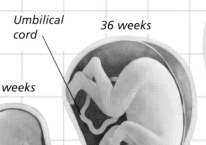
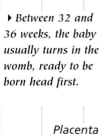

In the womb

Inside the uterus the single fertilized egg divides into two cells, then four, eight and so on. After a week it is a ball of a few hundred cells that buries itself in the blood-rich lining of the uterus and takes in nourishment for continued growth. After one month it is hardly larger than a rice grain, but the brain and heart are formed. After two months the tiny baby is still smaller than a thumb, yet all its main parts and organs have formed.

▶▶ **Read further > organs** pg8 (j14)

Sperm

Egg cell cytoplasm

Egg cell's outer coat

Getting together

The egg cell is only able to join with a sperm for a few days when a woman is ovulating (when an egg has been released from the ovary). Thousands of sperm cells swim near to the egg in the oviduct, but only one can join with or fertilize it. Both the egg and sperm contain sets of the body's genetic material, made of DNA *(see pg11 [n33])*. At fertilization the sets combine to form a unique set of genes for the new baby.

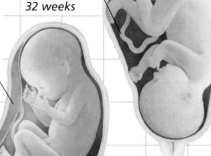

Egg cell nucleus

▶▶ **Read further > DNA** pg11 (b30)

▲ *An ultrasound scan shows the baby growing inside the womb.*

Nucleus with genetic material

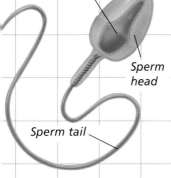

Sperm head

Sperm tail

▲ *Only one sperm can fertilize the released egg.*

▸ *A newborn baby is carefully checked by a doctor to ensure it is healthy.*

New life

In the womb it was warm, wet and quiet, and oxygen and food came direct from the mother into the baby's blood. At birth a baby is pushed and squeezed into the fresh air, lights and sounds of the outside world. The baby takes its first gasps of air, often crying as it does so. This is a good sign, since it opens up the baby's airways and lungs *(see pg18 [m11])*. These were not used in the womb, but now the baby must breathe to get oxygen for itself. It also needs food and soon the baby takes a first meal of its mother's milk. The milk provides all the nourishment it needs for the first months of its life.

▶▶ **Read further > nourishment** pg22 (d2)

Glossary

Alveoli Microscopic air spaces inside the lungs, with more than 300 million in each.

Antibodies Chemicals produced to attack a particular germ, known as an antigen.

Arteries Main blood vessels or tubes that carry blood away from the heart.

Bases In the genetic material DNA, types of chemical subunits that carry information in the form of a chemical code.

Bile A fluid containing waste products produced by the liver, stored in the gall bladder, and emptied into the small intestine.

Capillaries The smallest types of blood vessels, much thinner than human hairs, with walls only one cell thick.

Cells Microscopic parts of the body, like 'living building-blocks', which make up its tissues, organs and other parts.

Chromosomes Lengths of the genetic material DNA that have been coiled up very tightly to resemble microscopic threads.

Cilia Tiny flexible hairs, usually sticking out or projecting from a cell, that can bend or wave, or detect certain chemicals.

Cortex The outer region or layer of a body part such as the kidney, brain or lymph node.

DNA De-oxyribonucleic acid, a chemical that makes up the instructions or genes for how the body grows and functions.

Excretion Removal of wastes, by-products and other unwanted substances from the body – by the excretory or urinary system.

Gastric To do with the stomach, for example gastric juices made in the stomach contain powerful chemicals for digestion.

Genes Instructions or information, in the form of the chemical DNA, for how the body develops, grows and functions.

Genome The full set of all the genes for a human body, which number about 35,000.

Gland A body part specialized to make a certain product, usually in liquid form, which can be released directly into the blood flowing through the gland (endocrine gland).

Glucose A type of high-energy sugar, often called 'blood sugar', that is broken down inside the cells of the body to release its energy, which powers the cell's life processes.

Hormones Natural body substances that control processes such as growth, how fast cells use energy, and the balance of water.

Involuntary In the muscle system, when a muscle works automatically without need for thought, rather than being controlled.

Lymph A pale fluid that collects between cells and oozes slowly to collect in tubes and lymph ducts, and flow through lymph nodes.

Marrow Soft, jelly-like substance in the middle of many bones, which makes new cells for the blood (red marrow) or stores energy and nutrients as fat (yellow marrow).

Medulla The inner or lower region of a body part such as the kidney or brain.

Metabolism All of the body's internal chemical processes that involve changing and breaking down, such as digestion, respiration and excretion.

Motor In the body, to do with muscles and movements, for example motor nerves carry signals from the brain to muscles to tell them when to contract and by how much.

Myofibres Muscle fibres, which are bundled together inside a muscle – 'myo-' is to do with muscles.

Neurons Nerve cells, specialized to receive and pass on information in the form of tiny electrical signals called nerve impulses.

Nucleus The central region or control centre of a cell, containing the genetic material DNA.

Nutrients Substances in digested food that are useful to the body, such as providing energy for growth and repair of body parts.

Organelles Cell parts, such as the nucleus or control centre, and the folded sheets of membranes called endoplasmic reticulum.

Organs Major parts of the body such as the heart, lungs or stomach, which are usually made of several different kinds of tissues.

Oxygen A gas making up one-fifth of air, which has no colour, taste or smell but is needed in continuing supplies by the body to break apart substances such as glucose.

Plasma The liquid part of blood without the microscopic cells (red cells, white cells and platelets).

Pulse rate The number of times per minute that the heart beats and sends blood, causing pulsations (pressure waves) in the arteries.

REM sleep Rapid eye movement sleep, when body processes speed up slightly compared to deep sleep, and dreams usually occur.

Synapse The junction or connection between two nerve cells or neurons.

System Several parts such as tissues and organs that work together to carry out one major, vital function.

Tendon A strong, rope-like part where the end of a muscle narrows to join to a bone.

Tissues Parts of the body formed of many cells of the same kind, such as muscle cells (fibres) that make up muscle tissue.

Veins Main blood vessels or tubes that carry blood towards the heart.

Voluntary In the muscle system, when a muscle can be controlled at will or by thinking, rather than working automatically without the need for thought (involuntary).

Index

The publishers would like to thank the following
artists who have contributed to this book:
June Allan, Janos Marffy, Helen Parsley,
Martin Sanders, Mike Saunders, Rudi Vizi

All other photographs are from:
Corel, DigitalSTOCK, PhotoDisc

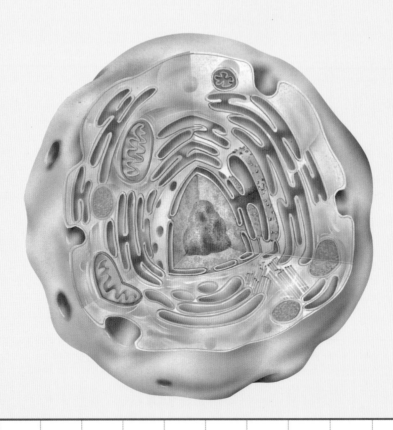